MIRRORS was first performed by the Greenroom Dramatic Society of Malden High School, Malden, Massachusetts, at Emerson College in Boston on February 6, 1982, with the following cast:

Fred Peterson	Walter Prince
Freddie Peterson	Dennis Boyd
Chip Peterson	Paul Nelson
Marita Peterson	Laurie Ross
Mrs. Peterson	Angela DeVito
Doctor	Jenifer Cosgrove
Stage Manager	Chris Nelson
Props	Sean Warren
Director	John O'Brien

MIRRORS was the winner of the 1982 Emerson College Award for outstanding theatrical achievement.

The community theatre premiere of *MIRRORS* was presented by the M.I.T. Players of Cambridge, Massachusetts, at Brandeis University in Waltham, Massachusetts in May, 1982.

MIRRORS
A One-Act Play
For Three Women and Three Men

CHARACTERS

FRED PETERSON . . . . .age forty

FREDDIE PETERSON. . . . . .Fred's son, age eighteen

CHIP PETERSON . . . . .Fred's other son, age sixteen

MARITA PETERSON . . . . Fred's daughter, age fourteen

MOTHER . . . . Fred's wife, age forty

DOCTOR. . . . . female, any age

Time: That is the question.

Place: Inside Fred Peterson's head

MIRRORS

A One-Act Play

By

JOHN O'BRIEN

THE DRAMATIC PUBLISHING COMPANY

*** NOTICE ***

The amateur and stock acting rights to this work are controlled exclusively by THE DRAMATIC PUBLISHING COMPANY without whose permission in writing no performance of it may be given. Royalty fees are given in our current catalogue and are subject to change without notice. Royalty must be paid every time a play is performed whether or not it is presented for profit and whether or not admission is charged. A play is performed anytime it is acted before an audience. All inquiries concerning amateur and stock rights should be addressed to:

DRAMATIC PUBLISHING
P. O. Box 129, Woodstock, Illinois 60098.

COPYRIGHT LAW GIVES THE AUTHOR OR THE AUTHOR'S AGENT THE EXCLUSIVE RIGHT TO MAKE COPIES. This law provides authors with a fair return for their creative efforts. Authors earn their living from the royalties they receive from book sales and from the performance of their work. Conscientious observance of copyright law is not only ethical, it encourages authors to continue their creative work. This work is fully protected by copyright. No alterations, deletions or substitutions may be made in the work without the prior written consent of the publisher. No part of this work may be reproduced or transmitted in any form or by any means, electronic or mechanical, including photocopy, recording, videotape, film, or any information storage and retrieval system, without permission in writing from the publisher. It may not be performed either by professionals or amateurs without payment of royalty. All rights, including but not limited to the professional, motion picture, radio, television, videotape, foreign language, tabloid, recitation, lecturing, publication, and reading are reserved. *On all programs this notice should appear:*

"Produced by special arrangement with
THE DRAMATIC PUBLISHING COMPANY of Woodstock, Illinois"

©MCMLXXXII by
JOHN O'BRIEN

Printed in the United States of America
All Rights Reserved
(MIRRORS)

ISBN 0-87129-540-7

MIRRORS

SCENE: The stage is in darkness. A match flares. We see a man's face. He stares into the flame. He blows out the match. After a short beat, lights come up on the man, FRED PETERSON, sitting in a rocking chair DC. He stares into space. FREDDIE PETERSON enters UR. The stage lights turn red.)

FREDDIE. Hey, Pop.
FRED (still in his reverie). Good morning.
FREDDIE. Morning? It's evening.
FRED (coming to life). Good evening.
FREDDIE. Do you know where the bicycle pump is?
FRED. It's in the cellar.
FREDDIE. You always know where everything is.
FRED. What else are fathers for? (FREDDIE exits DR. FRED continues to stare straight out and up.)

(CHIP enters UR, dressed to kill, except that he wears sneakers.)

CHIP. Hey, Father Fred.
FRED. Good evening. (CHIP stands atop the milk carton at DRC.)
CHIP. So tell me.
FRED. What do you want to know?
CHIP. Can't you guess?
FRED. It's in the cellar.

CHIP. What is?
FRED. The bicycle pump.
CHIP. I don't want the bicycle pump.
FRED. Just teasing.
CHIP. I want to know how I look.
FRED. Not bad.
CHIP. Not bad?
FRED. But I'm no expert.
CHIP. I look irresistible.
FRED. You need a second opinion.
CHIP. Who?
FRED. Someone wise in the ways of the world.
CHIP. Nobody's wiser than you, Pop. (He jumps off the carton.)
FRED. I have it.
CHIP. Who?
FRED. Your sister.
CHIP. Marita?
FRED. Do you have any others?
CHIP. What does she know about men's clothes?
FRED. She's a she.
CHIP. So?
FRED. Shes know everything about hes.
CHIP. Everything?
FRED. Everything worth knowing.
CHIP. I'll ask her. (He exits UC. FRED continues staring out and up.)

(MARITA enters UR.)

MARITA. Hi, Pop.
FRED. Hi, baby.
MARITA. I'm not a baby.
FRED. I keep forgetting.
MARITA. Have you seen Freddie?
FRED. Yes. (Pause.)

MIRRORS

MARITA. You're a tease.
FRED. He's in the cellar.
MARITA. What's he doing down there?
FRED. Looking for the bicycle pump.
MARITA. Thanks. (She starts to exit DR.)
FRED. I forgot to tell you.
MARITA. What?
FRED. Chip is looking for you.
MARITA. What for?
FRED. He wants to ask you how he looks.
MARITA. Why me?
FRED. I told him you're the best judge.
MARITA. Of what?
FRED. Of how a man looks.

(FREDDIE enters DR with the bicycle pump.)

FREDDIE. I found it.
MARITA. I am?
FRED. That's my boy.
FREDDIE. You are what?
MARITA. The best judge of how Chip looks.
FREDDIE. If you say so.
MARITA (pointing to FRED). He says so.
FREDDIE (pointing to FRED). If you say so.
MARITA. Is that all you can say?
FREDDIE. No.
MARITA. Then say something else.
FREDDIE. Good-bye.
MARITA. Very funny.
FRED. That's my boy.
FREDDIE. I'm going for a spin on my bike.
MARITA. Don't be late for supper.
FRED. I thought you wanted to see him.
MARITA. Who?

FRED. Freddie.
MARITA. I did?
FRED. You said you did.
MARITA. You're right, I did. I remember.
FREDDIE. What about?
MARITA. I forget.
FRED. That's my girl.

(CHIP enters UC.)

CHIP. Hi. (He stands on top of the carton.)
MARITA. 'Lo. He's high, I'm low.
FREDDIE. That's your offspring.
FRED. I can't keep up with them.
CHIP. How do I look? (MARITA notices his sneakers.)
MARITA. Almost perfect.
CHIP. What do you mean, almost?
MARITA. Nobody's perfect.
CHIP. Who says?
MARITA. My English teacher.
FREDDIE. I'll bet she thinks she's perfect.
MARITA. Who?
FREDDIE. Your English teacher.
MARITA. She's a him.
CHIP. She's a he.
FREDDIE (in mock amazement). Men teach English?
MARITA (appealing for help). Dad?
FRED. They're teasing you.
MARITA. I know that.
FREDDIE. And we only tease people we like.
MARITA. Flatterer.
CHIP. Come on, you can help me straighten my tie.
MARITA. It is straight. (CHIP pulls his bow tie to one side.)
CHIP. It was.

MARITA. I'm glad I'm not a boy.
FREDDIE. Me, too.
CHIP Let's go. (MARITA steps close to the milk carton and CHIP climbs on her back.)
MARITA. Lucky me. (She carries him piggyback off UR.)
FRED. To be young again.
FREDDIE. Was I that silly?
FRED. When?
FREDDIE. When I was young.
FRED. When *you* were young?
FREDDIE. When I was Chip's age.
FRED. No.
FREDDIE. Good.
FRED. You didn't get silly until later.
FREDDIE. I don't feel silly now.
FRED. Weren't you going for a spin?
FREDDIE. I was.
FRED. Change your mind?
FREDDIE. Yes.
FRED. It's a free country.
FREDDIE. So far.
FRED. What happened?
FREDDIE. When?
FRED. Just now.
FREDDIE. What do you mean?
FRED. Something must have happened to make you change your mind.
FREDDIE. Nothing happened.
FRED. If you say so.
FREDDIE. It's just that, when I was in the cellar, I got thinking about something.
FRED. That's my boy.
FREDDIE. Something I've thought about before.
FRED. The mystery deepens.
FREDDIE. And now's my chance.

FRED. For what?
FREDDIE. To see you alone . . . (He steps DR, puts the bicycle pump down.)
FRED. Here I am.
FREDDIE. And get some advice. (He sits on the milk carton.)
FRED. What else are fathers for?
FREDDIE. It's something that worries me.
FRED. Money?
FREDDIE. No.
FRED. Girls?
FREDDIE. No.
FRED. Heaven and hell?
FREDDIE. No.
FRED. Am I getting warm?
FREDDIE. No.
FRED. If I can't get warm with hell, I give up.
FREDDIE. It's gonna sound funny. I don't know if anyone else ever thought of it . . .
FRED. Probably not.
FREDDIE. Since the beginning of time.
FRED. The suspense is killing me.
FREDDIE. Are you ready?
FRED. I've been ready for five minutes.
FREDDIE. What do people do?
FRED. Did you say what I think you said?
FREDDIE. What do you think I said?
FRED. What do people do?
FREDDIE. That's what I said.
FRED. I don't get you.
FREDDIE. When I was young . . .
FRED. When *you* were young?
FREDDIE. When I was Chip's age.
FRED. Yes?
FREDDIE. I used to live.
FRED. What are you doing now?

MIRRORS Page 11

FREDDIE. I'm thinking.
FRED. That's dangerous.
FREDDIE. And I'm wondering what people do.
FRED. You don't mean their jobs?
FREDDIE. No.
FRED. I didn't think you did.
FREDDIE. I mean hour by hour.
FRED. Minute by minute.
FREDDIE. Second by second.
FRED. They bowl, they knit, they contemplate their navels, they scheme, they dream, they pour their drinks and bore their shrinks . . .
FREDDIE. Or their children.
FRED. They make love, they make hate, they think about yesterday, they think about tomorrow . . .
FREDDIE. What about today?
FRED. My son, the philosopher.
FREDDIE. I just started wondering about it a couple of weeks ago.
FRED. When you were brushing your teeth.
FREDDIE. How did you know?
FRED. That's when most great ideas come.
FREDDIE. Maybe I should brush my teeth three times a day.
FRED. It has to be in the morning.
FREDDIE. Do *you* have great ideas?
FRED. I always have great ideas.
FREDDIE. When you brush your teeth?
FRED. And when I wake up in the middle of the night.
FREDDIE. Me, too.
FRED. Do you know why?
FREDDIE. No.
FRED. That's when we're closest to our dreams.
FREDDIE. Or our nightmares.
FRED. They're even better.
FREDDIE. Nightmares are better than dreams?

FRED. More important.
FREDDIE. Do you have nightmares?
FRED. Doesn't everybody?
FREDDIE. I don't know.
FRED. Everybody has them. Some don't remember them.
FREDDIE. Do you remember yours?
FRED. I remember the ones I remember.
FREDDIE. What are they? (FRED stands and crosses DLC.)
FRED. One is about fire.
FREDDIE. Fire?
FRED. That's my favorite.
FREDDIE. What happens?
FRED. The house is on fire. You guys are burning.
FREDDIE. The family?
FRED. And I can't get you out.
FREDDIE. Jesus.
FRED. It haunts me.
FREDDIE. Is that your worst one?
FRED. There are two worse than that.
FREDDIE. How can anything be worse than that? (He crosses UC of the chair.)
FRED. You guys are burning, and I *can* get you out.
FREDDIE. Why is that worse?
FRED. I stand outside and watch you die.
FREDDIE. Why?
FRED. I'm afraid.
FREDDIE. What's your worst one?
FRED. I set the fire.
FREDDIE. And that's when you have your best thoughts?
FRED. Then and when I'm brushing my teeth.
FREDDIE. What happens when you brush your teeth?
FRED. I understand my nightmares.
FREDDIE. *Do* you understand them? (He crosses DLC to Fred's right.)
FRED. Yes.

MIRRORS   Page 13

FREDDIE. What do they mean?
FRED. That I'm afraid.
FREDDIE. Of fire?
FRED. Of myself.
FREDDIE. That you're going to kill?
FRED. That part of me wants to kill.
FREDDIE. What does it want to kill?
FRED. The other part. (FREDDIE sits in the chair.)
FREDDIE. So that's what people do.
FRED. The smart ones.
FREDDIE. They listen to their dreams.
FRED. And their nightmares.

(CHIP enters UR, wearing "regular" shoes.)

FREDDIE. Thanks for the advice.
FRED. I'll send you my bill in the morning.
CHIP. Anybody I know?
FREDDIE. What are you talking about?
CHIP. William.
FREDDIE. Who?
CHIP. He'll send you his "bill" in the morning.
FRED. That's my boy.
FREDDIE. Tell me he didn't say that . . .
CHIP. My turn.
FREDDIE. Not my brother.
FRED. What for?
CHIP. Advice.
FRED. I should charge by the hour.
FREDDIE. Do you want me to go?
FRED. That's up to Chip.
CHIP. You can stay.
FREDDIE. This is my lucky day.
FRED. Two Freds are better than one.
FREDDIE. Tell me he didn't say that . . .

FRED. Couldn't resist.
FREDDIE. Not my father.
CHIP. I gotta remember that one.
FREDDIE. Two of a kind.
FRED. I'm just a block off the young Chip.
FREDDIE. Oh, no.
CHIP. You're hot today, Pop.
FRED. Hot as a firecracker.
FREDDIE. Will both of you please act my age?
FRED. We'll try.
CHIP (to FREDDIE). Whatever you say, old man. (FREDDIE stands and crosses DRC to Chip's left.)
FREDDIE. What's your problem?
CHIP. I don't have any problem.
FREDDIE. What did you want to ask Pop?
CHIP. That's not a problem.
FREDDIE. What is it?
CHIP. It's a question.
FREDDIE. Okay, I'll string along. What's your question?
CHIP. I'm in love.
FREDDIE. Again?
FRED. That's not a question.
FREDDIE. And you want to know what love is.
CHIP. I know what it is.
FRED. You do?
FREDDIE. What is it?
CHIP. I want to know what it means.
FRED. Trouble.
CHIP. Is that all?
FRED. No. Not all.
CHIP. I want to know how I can be sure.
FRED. Of what?
CHIP. That this is it.
FREDDIE. It?
FRED (to FREDDIE). Do you want to try this one?

MIRRORS   Page 15

CHIP (to FRED). I didn't ask him.
FREDDIE. What's wrong with me?
CHIP. I asked him.
FREDDIE (to FRED). He asked you.
FRED. How can you be sure?
CHIP. Right.
FREDDIE. You can't.
CHIP. I didn't ask you.
FREDDIE. You asked him.
FRED. I think I know what's behind your question.
CHIP. Nothing's behind it.
FREDDIE. Something's behind everything. (He circles behind CHIP, trying to look sinister.)
CHIP. What's behind it?
FRED. You have someone special . . .
FREDDIE (speaking over Chip's shoulder). Of course he does. Why do you think he's dressed that way?
CHIP. What way?
FREDDIE. Up. (He squeezes the back of Chip's collar and leads CHIP toward the chair.)
FRED. But you keep thinking of others.
CHIP. How did you know that?
FREDDIE. Because you're human, Bozo. (He drops CHIP into the chair.)
FRED. And you think you're different.
CHIP. There must be something wrong with me.
FREDDIE. There is.
CHIP. What?
FREDDIE. You're stupid.
FRED. He means you don't understand yourself.
CHIP (crossing DLC to Fred's right). That doesn't mean I'm stupid.
FRED. Of course it doesn't.
CHIP. Is that all you can tell me?
FRED. I haven't told you anything.

CHIP. Yes, you have.
FRED. What?
CHIP. That I can't be sure.
FREDDIE. You didn't know that?
FRED. You can be sure.
CHIP. I can?
FREDDIE. He can?
CHIP. How?
FREDDIE. How?
FRED. When she is all women to you.
CHIP. All women?
FREDDIE. In one?
FRED. "Just as all rivers flow to the sea, you are all women to me."
FREDDIE (sitting in chair). That's good.
CHIP. Who said it?
FRED. I did.
FREDDIE. He means, who wrote it?
FRED. I did.
CHIP. When?
FRED. I wrote it to your mother, when we were young.
FREDDIE. It's beautiful.
FRED. Thank your mother. She inspired it.
CHIP. Did you really write it?
FRED (with mock amazement). You doubt your father?
CHIP. Just checking.
FREDDIE. Of course he wrote it, if he says he did.
FRED. The truth is, I have a crazy brother. I keep him chained in the attic, and during thunderstorms, I eavesdrop on his mad ravings.
CHIP. I guess I deserved that.
FREDDIE. Never try to go one up on Pop.
CHIP (crossing DL). "Just as all rivers ... "
FRED. "Flow to the sea."
CHIP. "You are ... "

MIRRORS Page 17

FRED. "All women to me."
CHIP. May I use it?
FRED. With your someone special?
CHIP. I'm gonna see her tonight.
FRED. You can use it on one condition.
CHIP. What's that?
FRED. If it's true.
CHIP. It's true.
FRED. Then it's all yours.
CHIP. What if she asks me who said it?
FRED. Tell her I did.
FREDDIE. He means, who wrote it?
FRED. Tell her you have a crazy father.

(MOTHER enters UR.)

FRED. You keep him chained in the attic.
MOTHER and FRED (together). And during thunderstorms . . . (FRED turns to face her.) . . . You eavesdrop on his mad ravings.
CHIP. You know about his crazy brother?
MOTHER. I should. He's been using that line for years.
FRED. Caught in the act.
CHIP. Anyway, thanks, Pop.
FRED. Any time.
CHIP. I gotta go. (He crosses DRC, right of FREDDIE in the chair and left of MOTHER.) I don't want to keep her waiting.
MOTHER. You're leaving now?
FREDDIE. Why do you think he's dressed that way?
MOTHER. What way?
FRED. Up.
FREDDIE. That's my father.
MOTHER. You'll miss supper.
CHIP. I'm taking her out to eat.
FRED. Good luck.

MOTHER. And don't slurp your soup.

CHIP. That's my mother. (FREDDIE reaches over and tugs at Chip's jacket. CHIP turns to face him.)

FREDDIE. If you do slurp your soup . . .

CHIP. I won't slurp my soup.

REDDIE. It will help you remember.

CHIP. Remember what? (FREDDIE puts his finger on Chip's neck and traces a meandering course down Chip's shirt.)

FREDDIE. The rivers that flow to the sea.

CHIP. That's my brother. (He exits DR.)

MOTHER. "You are all women to me."

FRED. You remembered that, too.

MOTHER. How could I forget?

FRED. He wanted to know the meaning of love.

FREDDIE. And Pop told him.

MOTHER. He should know.

FRED. If I don't know by now, I'm in trouble. (FREDDIE stands.)

FREDDIE. This is getting too mushy for me.

FRED. Mushy?

FREDDIE. I'm going outside. (He crosses DR.)

MOTHER. Don't go too far. (He picks up his bicycle pump.)

FREDDIE. Okay, Ma.

MOTHER. Supper will be ready soon. (FREDDIE exits DR.)

FRED. What's it like to be young?

MOTHER. Don't you remember? (She sits in the chair.)

FRED. He wanted to know about love. (He crosses upstage of chair.) Imagine that.

MOTHER. Did you know, when you were his age?

FRED. No.

MOTHER. Do you know now?

FRED. What do you think?

MOTHER. I think this is getting mushy.

FRED. Mushy. I wonder where he heard that.

MOTHER. Probably on late night T.V. "Andy Hardy Goes

to College."
FRED. That's my wife.
MOTHER. That's my husband. (FRED crosses DRC.)
FRED. Do you know something?
MOTHER. What? (FRED sits on the carton.)
FRED. They're better children to me than I was to my father.
MOTHER. What a silly thing to say.
FRED. It's not silly, it's true.
MOTHER. Maybe you're a better father to them.
FRED. I don't see how.
MOTHER. How are they better?
FRED. They confide in me.
MOTHER. I'm glad.
FRED. What a great thing that is.
MOTHER. They must have learned it somewhere.
FRED. From you, not from me.
MOTHER. Why do you always put yourself down?
FRED. Because I know myself better than anyone else does.
MOTHER. We all know ourselves better than anyone else.
FRED. I can't speak for anyone else.
MOTHER. Nobody can. (FRED crosses upstage of chair.)
FRED. So, speaking for myself, I am . . .
MOTHER. You are what?
FRED. Are you sure you want to know?
MOTHER. What else are wives for?
FRED. I am beyond . . .
MOTHER (teasingly). You're beyond belief.
FRED (crossing DL). I'm beyond forgiveness.
MOTHER (crossing DLC, to Fred's right). You're the dearest man I know.
FRED. Only because you don't know me.
MOTHER. If I don't, who does?
FRED. No one.
MOTHER. I'll take you just as you are.
FRED. I accept the offer.

MOTHER. Why are you beyond forgiveness?
FRED. I can't tell you.
MOTHER. Too personal?
FRED. Much.
MOTHER. Have you ever told anyone?

(MARITA enters UR.)

FRED. Look who's here.
MARITA. It's only me.
FRED. Why only?
MARITA (sitting in chair). Nobody important.
MOTHER (crossing upstage of chair). She's teasing you.
MARITA. What's doing?
FRED. I've been giving advice.
MARITA. Don't you ever need any?
MOTHER. That's my daughter.
FRED. I haven't needed advice since . . .
MARITA. Since when?
FRED. Since a long time ago.
MARITA. You need some now.
FRED. I do?
MARITA. Doesn't he?
MOTHER. Does he?
FRED. Do I?
MARITA. Your tie doesn't match your shirt.
MOTHER. Or vice versa.
FRED. Is a zebra white with black stripes or black with white stripes?
MOTHER. But we love you anyway.
MARITA. You're our favorite zebra.
FRED. Even a zebra can die of hunger.
MARITA. He's hinting.
MOTHER. How does a boiled dinner sound?
FRED. A dinner for supper?

MIRRORS

MARITA. That's my father.
FRED. I can shut my eyes and see it now.
MARITA. Why don't you shut your mouth and taste it?
FRED. That's my daughter. (MOTHER holds Marita's right ear between two fingers and lifts her from the chair.)
MOTHER. We'll call you when it's ready.
FRED. I'll be right here.
MARITA. Where else would he be? (MOTHER, still holding Marita's ear, leads her toward UR exit.)
FATHER. Drinking the air.
MOTHER. Don't drink too much.
MARITA. You'll get drunk. (MOTHER and MARITA exit UR.)
FRED (sitting in chair). That's my family. (He stares off into space.)

(The DOCTOR enters UL. Stage lights turn blue.)

DOCTOR. Good morning.
FRED. Good evening.
DOCTOR. Why do you say that?
FRED. I don't know.
DOCTOR. How are things by you?
FRED. All right.
DOCTOR. It's a beautiful sky.
FRED. My favorite time of year.
DOCTOR. Why?
FRED. The sun ...
DOCTOR. What about it?
FRED. Like a ball of fire.
DOCTOR. Yes.
FRED. It sets so late.
DOCTOR. And rises early.
FRED. Yes.
DOCTOR. You like long days?
FRED. Yes.

Page 22   **MIRRORS**

DOCTOR. And short nights.
FRED. Yes.
DOCTOR. Why?
FRED. More time to live.
DOCTOR. Less time to dream?
FRED. Yes.
DOCTOR. How are things at home?
FRED. Fine.
DOCTOR. The kids?
FRED. Great.
DOCTOR. Your wife?
FRED. She's all right.
DOCTOR. Where are you now?
FRED. On the porch.
DOCTOR. Where are they?
FRED. Different directions.
DOCTOR. Like what?
FRED. Freddie's outside, fixing his bicycle. Chip's out on a date. Marita and my wife are in the house.
DOCTOR. What are they doing?
FRED. Cooking supper.
DOCTOR. What's it going to be?
FRED. A boiled dinner. A dinner for supper.
DOCTOR. How soon will it be ready?
FRED. In a few minutes.
DOCTOR. Is that carton on the porch?
FRED. Yes. (As FRED watches apprehensively, the DOCTOR swings upstage of chair, crosses to the carton, picks it up and crosses DLC, where she puts the carton down.)
DOCTOR. Do you have time to talk?
FRED. I'd rather not.
DOCTOR. It's a free country. (She sits on the carton.)
FRED. So far. (Long beat. FRED stands and crosses DRC.) All right. (DOCTOR crosses to Fred's left.)
DOCTOR. Relax.

FRED. I'll try.
DOCTOR. Don't try. That'll make it worse.
FRED. What do I do?
DOCTOR. Try not to try.
FRED. I'm trying.
DOCTOR. Now I know you've heard this before.
FRED. Yes.
DOCTOR. Many times.
FRED. Too many.
DOCTOR. It's for your own good.
FRED. Is it?
DOCTOR. You know it is. (FRED crosses DLC.)
FRED. Yes.
DOCTOR. Ready on the right, ready on the left . . .
FRED. Fire.
DOCTOR. I . . .
FRED. I . . .
DOCTOR. Fred Peterson . . .
FRED. Fred Peterson . . .
DOCTOR. Want to live . . .
FRED. Want to live . . .
DOCTOR. In reality.
FRED. In reality.
DOCTOR. Now answer these questions.
FRED. That's enough.
DOCTOR. Are you alive? (FRED crosses to the Doctor's left. They face each other DRC.)
FRED. I have to go to supper.
DOCTOR. Are you alive?
FRED. Yes.
DOCTOR. Is your family alive?
FRED. Yes.
DOCTOR. Is your family alive? (FRED turns away from her.)
FRED. No.
DOCTOR. When did they die?

FRED. Long ago.

DOCTOR. How long? (FRED walks away from the DOCTOR, swinging upstage of the chair.)

FRED. I forget. (The DOCTOR follows him. She swings upstage of the chair, and both move in a figure-eight pattern to the left of the chair, finishing the swing in front of the chair.)

DOCTOR. One year, two years, three years, four years, five years...

FRED (turning to face her in front of the chair). Stop it.

DOCTOR. How long?

FRED. Ten years.

DOCTOR. How did they die?

FRED. In a house.

DOCTOR. *How* did they die?

FRED. In a fire.

DOCTOR. Where?

FRED. In a house.

DOCTOR. What house?

FRED. Their home.

DOCTOR. Your home.

FRED. Our home.

DOCTOR. How many died?

FRED. Five.

DOCTOR. How many?

FRED. Four.

DOCTOR. Who were they?

FRED. My family.

DOCTOR. *Who* were they?

FRED. My wife, my little boys, my baby girl.

DOCTOR. When did the fire start?

FRED. Ten years ago.

DOCTOR. *When* did it start?

FRED. In the middle of the night.

DOCTOR. Where were you?

FRED. In another town.

MIRRORS

DOCTOR. Another house?
FRED. Yes.
DOCTOR. Whose house?
FRED. Someone else's.
DOCTOR. Who? (FRED sits in the chair. The DOCTOR stands to the left of the chair.)
FRED. A woman. (The DOCTOR moves upstage of the chair.)
DOCTOR. How did you hear about the fire?
FRED. I woke up.
DOCTOR. When?
FRED. In the middle of the night.
DOCTOR. And?
FRED. I turned on the radio.
DOCTOR. Why?
FRED. I don't know.
DOCTOR. What did you do?
FRED. I turned on the radio.
DOCTOR. What did you do when you heard the news?
FRED. I came here.
DOCTOR (crossing DR). But you don't want to stay here forever, do you?
FRED. Why should I leave?
DOCTOR. To live.
FRED. What for?
DOCTOR. Don't you know?
FRED. Do you?
DOCTOR. Living *here and now* is all we have.
FRED. It's all you have.
DOCTOR. It's all anybody has.
FRED. How do you know?
DOCTOR. I know.
FRED. That's no answer.
DOCTOR. And so do you.
FRED. How do you know what I know?
DOCTOR. Do you want me to leave you alone?

FRED. Yes.

DOCTOR. Enjoy your supper. (She crosses UL, intending to exit.)

FRED. Don't go. (The DOCTOR stops, comes DL.)

DOCTOR. All right.

FRED. Make me say it again.

DOCTOR. No.

FRED. Please.

DOCTOR. Say it yourself.

FRED. Alone?

DOCTOR. We're born alone, we die alone.

FRED. I can't.

DOCTOR. I . . .

FRED. I . . .

DOCTOR. Don't stop now.

FRED. Fred Peterson . . .

DOCTOR. It's you against the universe.

FRED. Want to live in reality. I am alive. My family is dead. They died in a fire ten years ago . . . my wife, my little boys, my baby girl. It started in the middle of the night. There was no one to help them. I was in another town, another house, with another woman.

DOCTOR (moving to Fred's left). That was the first time.

FRED. What was?

DOCTOR. The first time you ever said it by yourself.

FRED. Yes.

DOCTOR. How did it feel?

FRED. It hurt.

DOCTOR. Now comes the hardest part of all. (FRED stands and crosses DRC.)

FRED. No more.

DOCTOR (crossing to Fred's left). You must forgive yourself.

FRED. No. (He squeezes his eyes shut.)

DOCTOR. You must.

FRED. I can't.

MIRRORS

DOCTOR. Look at me.
FRED (opening his eyes). I'm looking.
DOCTOR. Do you think I never hurt anyone?
FRED. You?
DOCTOR. Do you think I never did anything I'm ashamed of?
FRED. I don't know.
DOCTOR. I do.
FRED. You're not me.
DOCTOR. We must all forgive ourselves.
FRED. I can't.
DOCTOR. You will.
FRED. Never.
DOCTOR. Never is a long, long time. (FRED crosses DLC and sits on the carton. When he speaks, he sounds like a new man.)
FRED. Doctor?
DOCTOR. Yes?
FRED. Did I ever thank you?
DOCTOR. You don't have to.
FRED. I want to.
DOCTOR. Go ahead.
FRED. Thank you.
DOCTOR. You're welcome.
FRED (looking skyward). Will you stay awhile, to watch the sun come up?
DOCTOR. Sorry.
FRED. Other patients?
DOCTOR. You're not the only ...
FRED. Loony in the bin?
DOCTOR. I wasn't going to say that.
FRED. I know.
DOCTOR (crossing to Fred's right). I'll let you in on a secret.
FRED. I love secrets.
DOCTOR. You're going to make it. (FRED stands.)
FRED. If I do, I'll owe it to you.
DOCTOR. See you tomorrow. (She exits UL. FRED crosses C stage and sits in the chair.)

FRED. That's my doctor. (He stares at the sun.)

(MOTHER enters UR. Stage lights turn red. She crosses upstage of chair and speaks to FRED from his left.)

MOTHER. Fred? (He doesn't respond. She moves further upstage of chair and speaks to him from his right.) Fred? (He snaps out of his reverie.)
FRED. What? Oh, it's you.
MOTHER. Only me.
FRED. Don't say that.
MOTHER. Were you with her?
FRED. Who?
MOTHER. The doctor.
FRED. Caught in the act.
MOTHER. Is she coming back?
FRED. Yes.
MOTHER. When?
FRED. Tomorrow morning. (MOTHER kneels by his right side.)
MOTHER. Fred?
FRED. What?
MOTHER. You are all men to me.
FRED. I don't deserve it.
MOTHER. You are the rivers that flow to the sea.
FRED. Thank you.
MOTHER. We're going to keep you here, where you belong. This is your home.
FRED. Thank you.
MOTHER. Fred?
FRED. What?
MOTHER. Tell me something?
FRED. If I can.
MOTHER. What did she say?
FRED. Who?
MOTHER. The doctor.

MIRRORS

FRED. The same as always.
MOTHER. The fire?
FRED. Yes.
MOTHER. Why is it always the fire?
FRED. I don't know.
MOTHER. You do know she's not real? (Long beat.)
FRED. Yes.
MOTHER. And we are.
FRED. Yes.
MOTHER. I'm glad.
MARITA (offstage). Supper's ready.
MOTHER. That means us. (She stands.)
FRED. I'll be right in.
MOTHER. It will get cold.
FRED. I just want to watch the sun go down.
MOTHER. We'll be waiting for you. (She exits UR. FRED stares at the sky.)

(The DOCTOR enters UL. Stage lights turn blue.)

DOCTOR. The nurse says you haven't had breakfast.
FRED. Breakfast?
DOCTOR. Blueberry pancakes. Your favorite.
FRED. I'll be right in.
DOCTOR. We'll be waiting for you. (She exits UL. FRED stares at the sky.)
MOTHER (offstage R). Supper. (Stage lights turn red. FRED stands, starts to exit UR. Just as he gets to the UR exit, he hears another voice.)
DOCTOR (offstage L). Breakfast. (Stage lights turn blue. FRED turns, starts to exit UL. Just as he gets to the UL exit, he hears another voice.)
MOTHER (offstage R). Boiled dinner. (Stage lights turn red. FRED turns, starts to exit UR. Just as he gets to the UR exit, he hears another voice.)

DOCTOR (offstage L). Blueberry pancakes. (Stage lights turn blue. This time, FRED runs across the stage, intending to exit UL. Just as he gets to the UL exit, he hears another voice.)

MOTHER (offstage R). We're waiting for you. (Stage lights turn red. FRED starts to exit UR. Just as he gets to the UR exit, he hears another voice.)

DOCTOR (offstage L). Come and get it. (Stage lights turn blue. FRED starts to exit UL. When he gets UC he stops, stares out at the sky, comes DC, takes a book of matches from his pocket, strikes a match. Blackout. In the darkness we see, as in the beginning, the face of FRED, staring into a flame. He blows out the match.)

THE END

PRODUCTION NOTES

A porch runs the length of the downstage area. It serves as the porch of a house at R and as the porch of a hospital at L.

The only props needed are cigarettes, matches and a bicycle pump. DC stage there is a rocking chair, and an upside down milk carton is at DRC. The costumes for the family should be ordinary street clothes. The doctor should be dressed appropriately.

At no time does Fred touch any of the other characters and they, in turn, do not touch him. They may touch each other.

When the Peterson family is on stage the stage lights are red. When the doctor comes on, stage lights turn to blue.

DIRECTORS NOTES